I0417373

It's Time to Say Goodnight

LINEWORK PATTERN WORKBOOK

by Annie Lang

Bubble baths, toothbrushes, bedtime stories, counting sheep, pillow play, a snuggle with teddy, a glass of water and then it's time to get tucked in and say goodnight! Choose from dozens of mix and match bedtime ritual and tooth fairy themed designs created from Annie's Bed 'n Bath, Sleepytime Bears, Happy Sheep and Toothfairies collection of images.

Simply trace the design and then transfer the image onto your project surface to make outstanding personalized items with professional results every time.

Copyright (C) Annie Lang 2016 anniethingspossible.com
The images in this book are intended for personal, classroom and small resale busisness use to create individually crafted items. Use for the creation of commercially manufactured/printed product items is strictly prohibited. Content in this publication. may not be duplicated or distributed for the purpose of electronic data file sharing either for free or for profit. Annie Lang retains all rights to the copyrighted properties in this publication and rights to any images cannot be claimed, reassigned or transferred to another party.

Transferring the linework designs

Trace the design of your choice with pencil and tracing paper. Place transfer paper under the tracing paper and place onto your selected surface. Hold in place with tape if necessary. Retrace over the linework to transfer the design onto the project. For fabrics, trace the design, flip the pattern over and retrace the lines using a fabric transfer pen. Follow manufacturer's direction to iron the design onto your chosen fabric item.

Color or paint these designs with

Craft paints, watercolors, markers, coloring pencils, chalks, inks, fabric pens, paint pens, or crayons

These designs are great for

Home Dec Items like furniture, cabinets, accent items, walls, lamps, glassware, kitchen accessories, office and desk items, bathroom accents, cabinets, patio pots and outdoor items, etc.
Fabric and wearable items like t-shirts, sweatshirts, aprons, canvas shoes, totes, quilting squares, table linens and napkins, window and shower curtains, pillows, etc.
Paper Craft Projects like greeting cards, scrap page elements, tags, labels, stationery items, ornaments, gift bags, etc.

For more ideas and designer tips, please visit my Blog at
http://annielang-anniethingspossible.blogspot.com/
My Pinterest Board at http://www.pinterest.com/anniethings/
or my Facebook Page at
http://www.facebook.com/anniethingspossible

anniethingspossible.com
creative designs by Annie Lang

Copyright (C) Annie Lang
www.anniethingspossible.com

Annie's
Bathtub
Babies

Copyright (C)
Annie Lang

Annie's
Bathtub
Babies

www.anniethingspossible.com

Annie's
Bubble Bath
Babies

Copyright (C) Annie Lang
www.anniethingspossible.com

Annie's
Scrub-a-Dub Girl

Copyright (C) Annie Lang
www.anniethingspossible.com

Annie's
Scrub-a-Dub Boy

Copyright (C) Annie Lang
www.anniethingspossible.com

Annie's
Toothbrushing
Girl

Copyright (C) Annie Lang
www.anniethingspossible.com

Copyright (C)
Annie Lang

Annie's
"All Tucked
In for
the Night"
Girl

www.anniethingspossible.com

Annie's
Toothbrushing
Boy

Copyright (C) Annie Lang
www.anniethingspossible.com

Annie's "All Tucked In for the Night" Boy

Copyright (C) Annie Lang
www.anniethingspossible.com

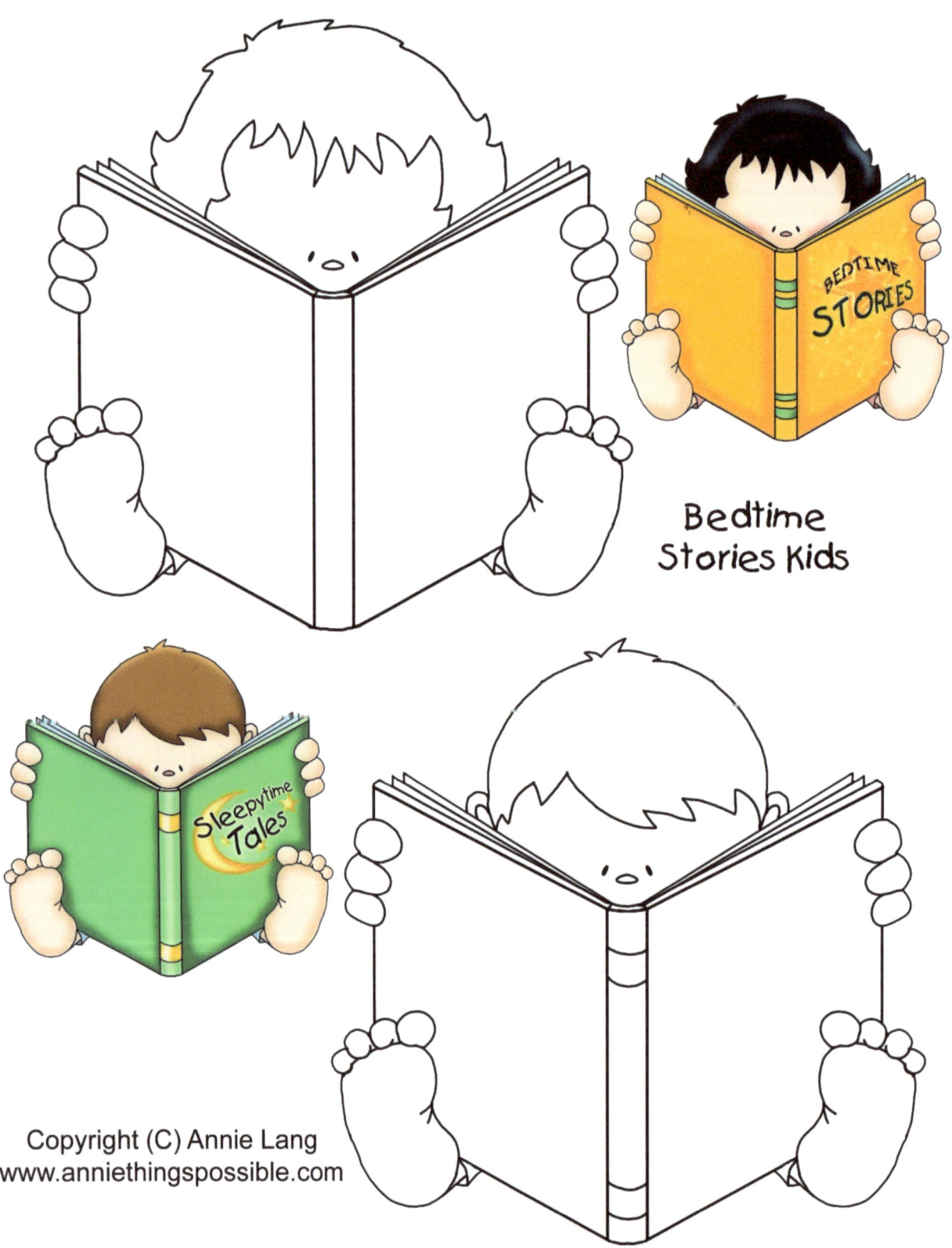

Bedtime
Stories Kids

Copyright (C) Annie Lang
www.anniethingspossible.com

ANNIE'S
HAPPY SHEEP

Copyright (C) Annie Lang   www.anniethingspossible.com

ANNIE'S
HAPPY SHEEP

Copyright (C) Annie Lang
www.anniethingspossible.com

ANNIE'S
HAPPY SHEEP

Copyright (C) Annie Lang
www.anniethingspossible.com

ANNIE'S
HAPPY SHEEP
Copyright (C) Annie Lang
www.anniethingspossible.com

Copyright (C) Annie Lang   www.anniethingspossible.com

ANNIE'S
HAPPY SHEEP

Copyright (C) Annie Lang
www.anniethingspossible.com

Sleepy
Midnight
Snacker
Bear

Copyright (C) Annie Lang   www.anniethingspossible.com

Sleepy Bedtime Bear

Copyright (C) Annie Lang   www.anniethingspossible.com

Sleepy Hugger Bears

Copyright (C) Annie Lang
www.anniethingspossible.com

Sleepy
Hand Stand
Bear

Copyright (C) Annie Lang   www.anniethingspossible.com

Sleepy
Pillow
Jumping
Bear

Copyright (C) Annie Lang
www.anniethingspossible.com

Copyright (C) Annie Lang
www.anniethingspossible.com

Sleepy
Pillow Tossing
Bear

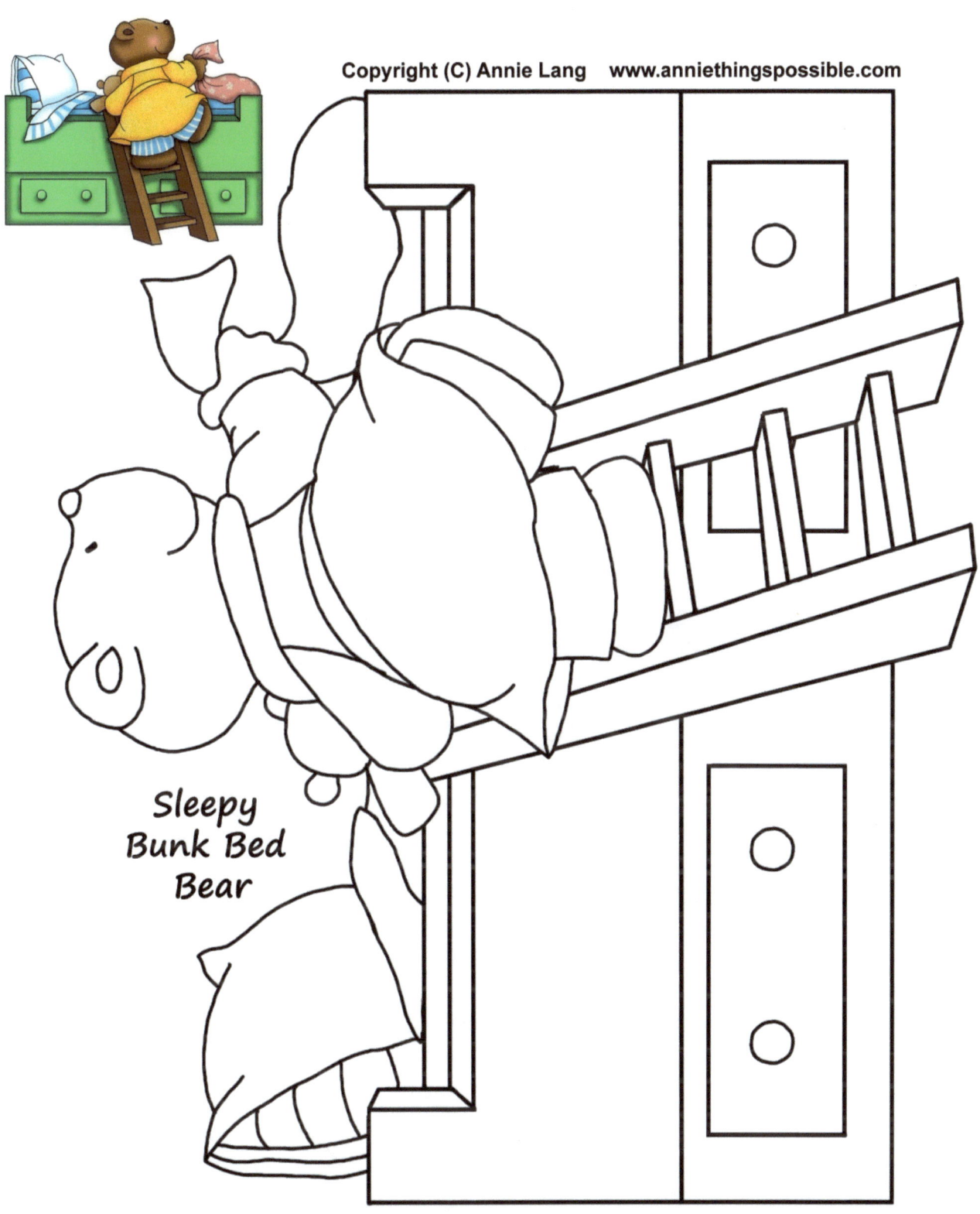

Sleepy
Bunk Bed
Bear

Copyright (C) Annie Lang   www.anniethingspossible.com

Sleepy
Yawning
Bears

Copyright (C) Annie Lang   www.anniethingspossible.com

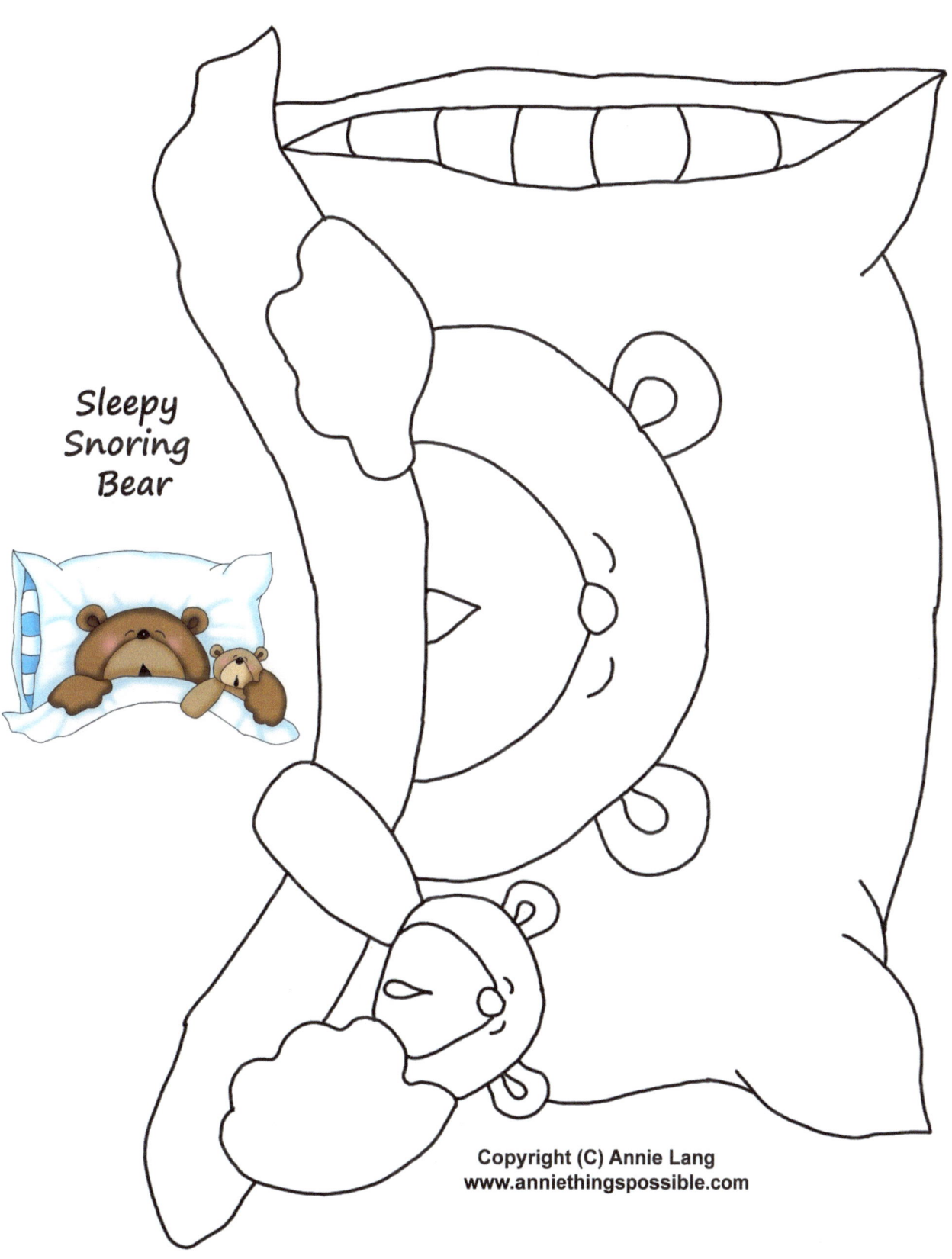

Sleepy
Snoring
Bear

Copyright (C) Annie Lang
www.anniethingspossible.com

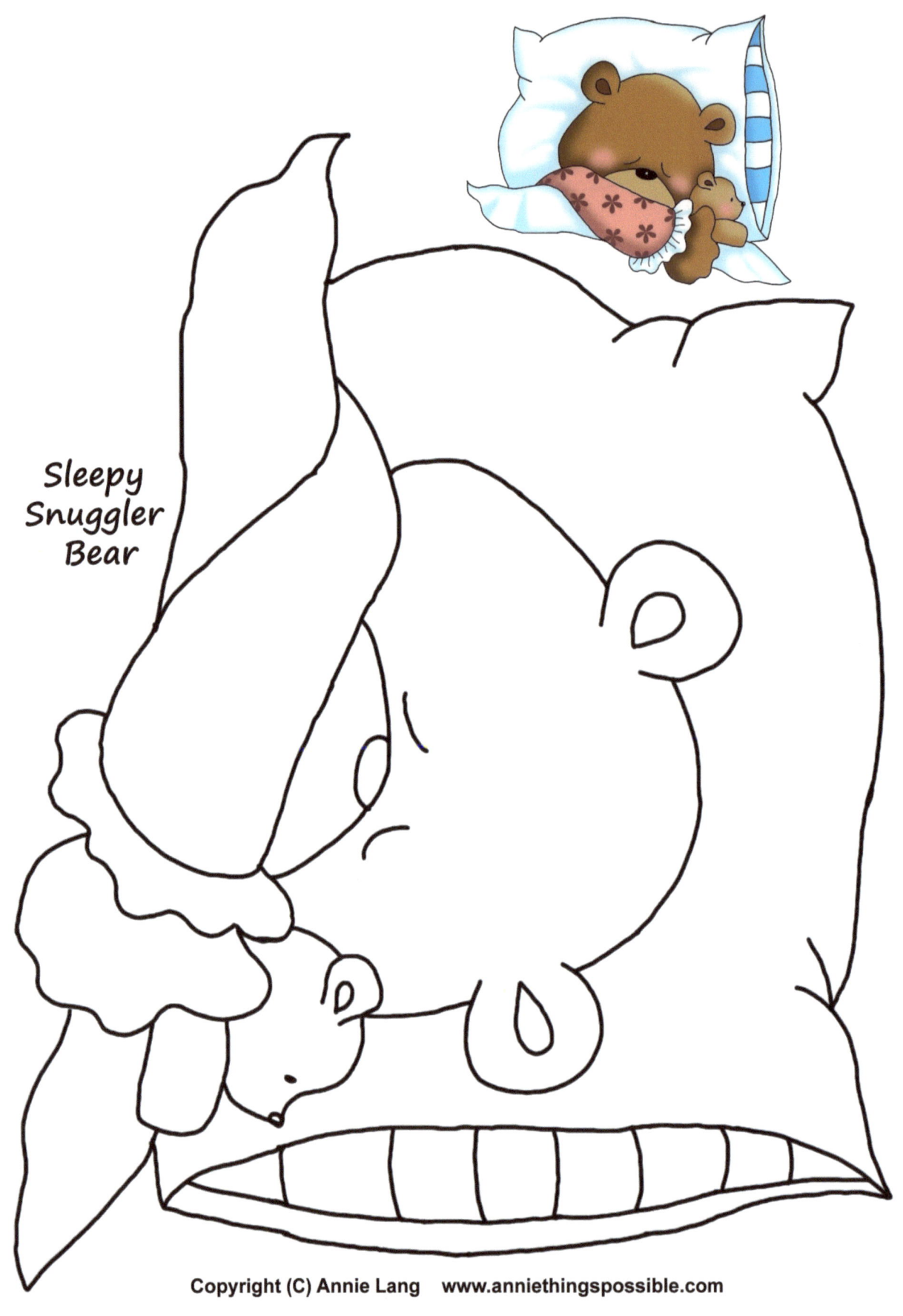

Sleepy
Snuggler
Bear

Copyright (C) Annie Lang   www.anniethingspossible.com

Copyright (C) Annie Lang
www.anniethingspossible.com

Sleepy
Thumb
Sucking
Bear

Sleepy Bear
Odds & Ends Motifs

Copyright (C) Annie Lang
www.anniethingspossible.com

Copyright (C) Annie Lang
www.anniethingspossible.com

Annie's Toothfairies

Copyright (C) Annie Lang
www.anniethingspossible.com

Annie's Toothfairies

Annie's Toothfairies

Copyright (C) Annie Lang
www.anniethingspossible.com

Annie's Toothfairies

Copyright (C) Annie Lang
www.anniethingspossible.com

*You can easily
personalize your
project by adding
a name or message
on the banner!

Annie's Toothfairies

Copyright (C) Annie Lang
www.anniethingspossible.com

Annie's Toothfairies

Copyright (C) Annie Lang
www.anniethingspossible.com

Copyright (C) Annie Lang
www.anniethingspossible.com

Annie's Toothfairies

my first tooth

my first tooth

Toothfairy

Annie's Toothfairies

Copyright (C) Annie Lang
www.anniethingspossible.com

Toothfairy

Happy Teeth make Happy Smiles

Happy Teeth make Happy Smiles

Smiles are universal!

Annie's Toothfairies

Copyright (C) Annie Lang
www.anniethingspossible.com

Smiles are universal!

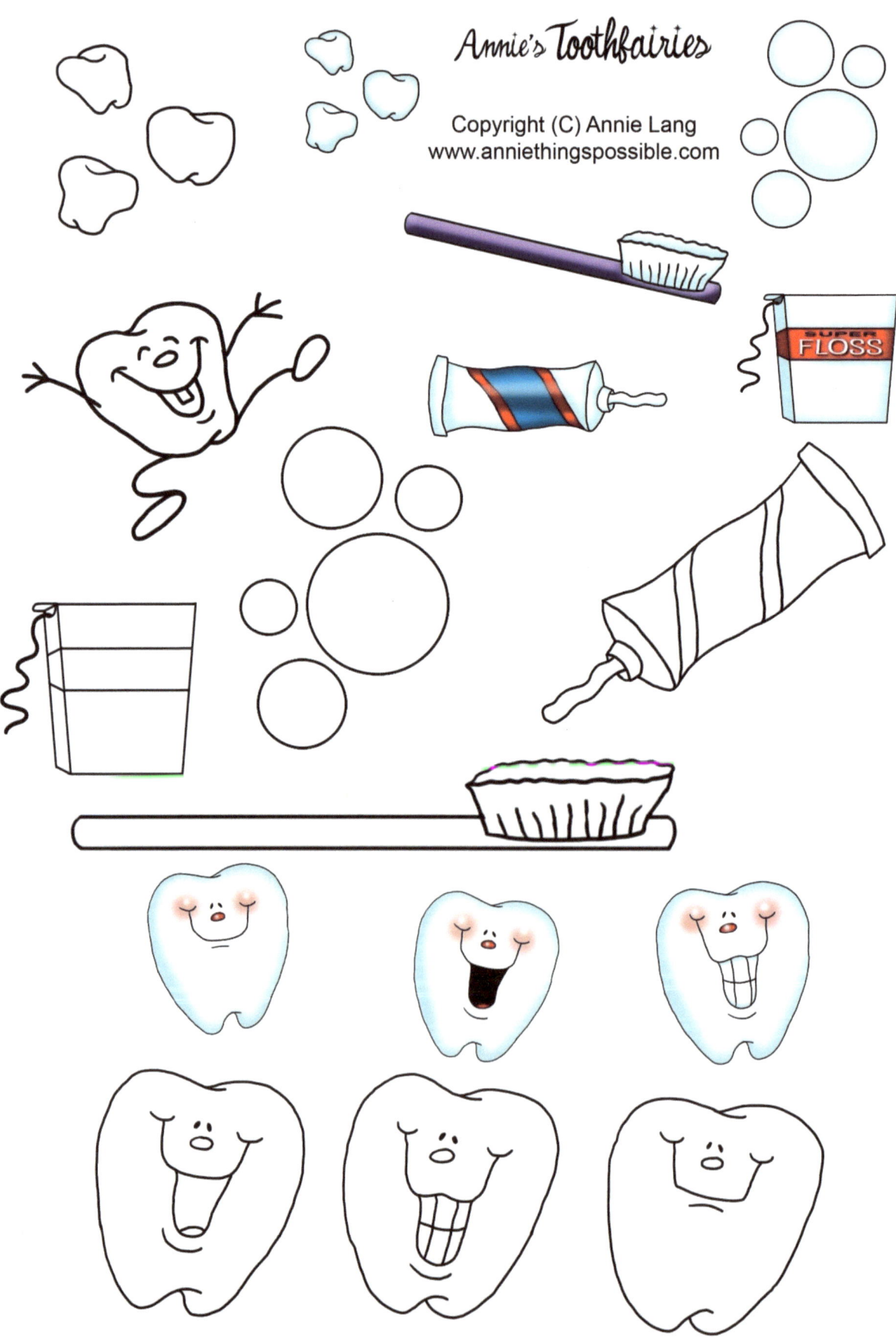

Annie's Toothfairies

Copyright (C) Annie Lang
www.anniethingspossible.com

notes and memos

anniethingspossible.com
creative designs by Annie Lang

Thank you for purchasing this publication!

Find dozens of other fun titles on my
Annie Lang's Books website!

Annie Lang's

books

Annie Lang characters, Annie Lang books, Annie Lang art , linework patterns and more!

http://annielangsbooks.com

...it's the place where Annie Things Possible!

*I hope you enjoyed this book and
encourage you to leave a review and share your
thoughts for other customers at Amazon.com!*

*To learn more about the author, get free project
ideas, see video how-to's and more, please visit
Annie Lang's BLOG at
http://annielang-anniethingspossible.blogspot.com/*

anniethingspossible.com
creative designs by Annie Lang

www.ingramcontent.com/pod-product-compliance
Lightning Source LLC
Chambersburg PA
CBHW041524280526

45792CB00004B/1365